The
Power
of
Travel

*A Passport
to Adventure,
Discovery,
and Growth*

**STEVE
ZIKMAN**

Most Tarcher/Putnam books are available at special quantity discounts for bulk purchases for sales promotions, premiums, fund-raising, and educational needs. Special books or book excerpts also can be created to fit specific needs. For details, write Putnam Special Markets, 375 Hudson Street, New York, NY 10014.

Jeremy P. Tarcher/Putnam
a member of
Penguin Putnam Inc.
375 Hudson Street
New York, NY 10014
www.penguinputnam.com

Library of Congress Cataloging-in-Publication Data

Zikman, Steve
The power of travel: a passport to adventure, discovery, and growth /
Steve Zikman.
p.   cm.
ISBN 0-87477-981-2 (alk. paper)
1. Self-actualization (Psychology)   2. Travel—Psychological aspects.
I. Title.
BF637.S4 Z55 1999
910'.01'9—dc21   99-17351 CIP Rev.

Printed in the United States of America

3   5   7   9   10   8   6   4   2

This book is printed on acid-free paper. ∞

Book design by Mauna Eichner

For my grandparents,

who set out on one great powerful journey

when they immigrated to Canada

seventy-five years ago

Getting There

Go

Freedom

Discovery

Summoning Our Senses
The Magnificence of the New
Time Changes
On the Wings of Serendipity
Travel Is Naïve and Wondrous
We Explore
Outward and Inward
We Rediscover

Encounter

People
Children
We Have Permission to
   Be a Stranger
Hospitality
Conversation
Friendship
We Return to Our New Friends
A Gift to Ourselves and Others
Travel Brings Us to Nature
We Capture Our Unique
   Encounters
We Are Nature's Witness
Our Special Spots
We Find New Places to Call Home

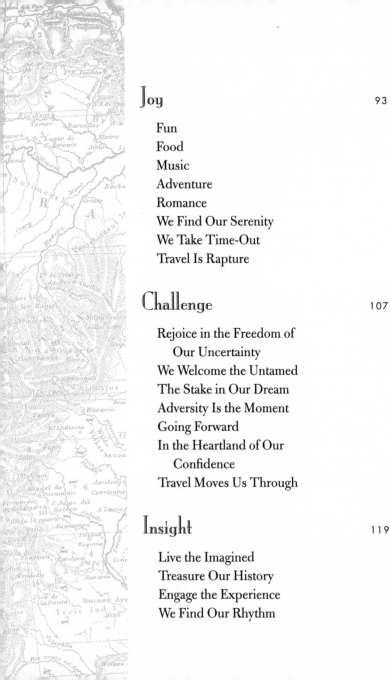

Growth

Savor the Power

More Power

The Power of Travel

Introduction

On the way home from the small Himalayan kingdom of Bhutan, I met with Mother Teresa. Not once, but twice.

My friend Laurie and I had flown into Calcutta from Paro in the early afternoon. We had one day in the City of Joy before she would fly on to Bangkok and I would return to Canada via New Delhi, Bombay, and London.

Over lunch, we toyed with the notion of visiting Mother Teresa's orphanage. A taxi ride and a couple of hours later, we were touched by the sight of forty or fifty little kids playing in a small courtyard, half of them running around completely undressed, the others in blue-and-white-striped outfits. As we were leaving, a Sister informed us that Mother Teresa was over in Mother House, only a few blocks away.

Within minutes we were standing in front of a rather inconspicuous wooden door with a

large cross on it. On a small, simple sign to the left of the door, in white lettering, were the modest words "Mother Teresa." When asked who we wished to see, we answered simply and in unison: "Mother Teresa." The Sister showed us in, and in a short while she returned with the words "Mother will meet with you."

We found ourselves waiting nervously on a plain bench, trying to figure out what we were going to say. Suddenly, from behind two swinging doors, we saw a white-and-blue sari and two old feet in open sandals. We gazed in awe as Mother Teresa moved briskly toward us. She sat next to Laurie, took her hand, and got right down to business.

She asked us where we were from and whether we were volunteers. She described the trip she had recently taken to Montréal. She told us that she was in a hurry, as she was leaving again the next day. With that, she got up, disappeared behind a screen partition, and quickly returned with two cards bearing her picture and a small prayer. She signed both—"God bless you. Teresa M.C."—and left. Though neither of us was religious, we sat there frozen, in a state of reverence.

But the story continues. Through a bizarre set of coincidences, I ended up meeting Mother Teresa again—thirty-six hours later, at three o'clock in the morning in the First Class lounge at Bombay airport while waiting for a delayed connecting flight.

She was sitting on a couch praying quietly by a small light. Everyone else was fast asleep. When I finally approached her and remarked that we had met just the day before in Calcutta, her wrinkled face strained upward to meet my puzzled eyes, and she quipped: "God works in mysterious ways." I smiled. She invited me to sit next to her.

We spent an hour discussing the scope and urgency of her work before she excused herself to return to her prayers. I withdrew to another couch, studying her every movement until I heard my flight being called for boarding. As I got up, so did she. Mother Teresa was on my flight.

On a quiet Sunday morning in Cape Town, I met Nelson Mandela.

I had just attended Desmond Tutu's last service as Archbishop. Walking back to my car along a quaint side street, I noticed a group of photographers waiting outside a small colonial building. Suddenly, all but one scurried off. I approached him. He suspected that Mandela was still in the building and would be coming out soon. So I waited.

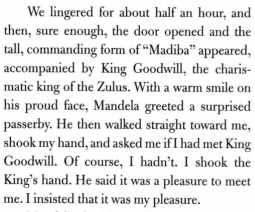

We lingered for about half an hour, and then, sure enough, the door opened and the tall, commanding form of "Madiba" appeared, accompanied by King Goodwill, the charismatic king of the Zulus. With a warm smile on his proud face, Mandela greeted a surprised passerby. He then walked straight toward me, shook my hand, and asked me if I had met King Goodwill. Of course, I hadn't. I shook the King's hand. He said it was a pleasure to meet me. I insisted that it was my pleasure.

Mandela, the King, and I chatted for a few moments as the photographer snapped a picture of me and Mandela shaking hands again. The camera jammed, and as I stood there hand in hand with this great leader, I tried to absorb the full magnificence of that moment of contact.

Travel has allowed my life's path to intersect with these two exceptional human beings. In fact, travel has blessed me with countless opportunities for adventure, discovery, and growth. Over the last fifteen years, I have explored and experienced life all around the world, through fifty-two countries and six continents.

For me, travel is watching the tide come in at Mont St. Michel. Enjoying a home-cooked meal at the home of people I had met only hours before. Visiting the village in Eastern Europe where my grandmother was born. Whitewater rafting down the Zambesi River.

Travel is listening to street musicians jam during an early-morning impromptu jazz session in a Paris club. Working on a sheep farm in New Zealand during lambing season. Shopping for a Chinese opera robe in Beijing. Driving through the countryside on a Sunday afternoon.

Travel is bar-hopping with locals in Krakow. Searching for mountain gorillas in the Zairean morning mist, hiking thirty kilometers to newly erupting volcanoes in the afternoon, and falling asleep that same evening in a local mission.

Travel is hitching a ride with ten Italians on the edge of the Kalahari and then being invited for a lunch of pasta, Italian bread, and wine out of the back of their Jeep. Visiting Elvis's grave at Graceland. Ringing in the New Year in a disco in the Ecuadorean jungle. Relaxing by a hotel pool.

I have always made the time and the space for travel. A weekend getaway. A one- or two-week vacation. Two or three months in Europe or Asia during my summer breaks. In fact, I left a lucrative practice as an attorney in a large Canadian law firm just to travel around the world for three years.

In the hours after I sent a memo to the associates and partners, informing them of my decision, I had a steady stream of colleagues pop their heads into my office, carefully shut the door behind them, and pull up one of my client chairs. Apparently impressed by my courage, they then proceeded to reveal their own secret plans, their own travel dreams.

Some had traveled before and were anxiously longing to return to the road. Others had never really traveled but hoped to do so soon. Still others confided in me that they wanted to get away for just a short while—a little rest, a brief sojourn, a few days, or a week. Although I seemed to be expected to abide by some unsworn vow of nomadic silence, I wondered why we suppress our irrepressible desire to travel.

From a young age, we are drawn to captivating far-off people and places. Our impetus to move, to stretch our horizons, to meet other people, to take that much-needed break is natural and powerful. Our desire to travel is strong, stronger than ever.

Technology has made the world smaller, more available, more accessible. We now have the ability to be almost anywhere in the world within twenty-four hours. Travel is cheaper, faster, easier. More countries are open to travelers than ever before.

Of course, travel is different for everyone. For some, it's a Caribbean cruise. For others, travel is a seven-day retreat, an organized month-long safari in Kenya, a six-week trek in Nepal, a year-long trip around the world with nothing but a backpack. Sometimes, travel is simply a couple of days in the next town, away from our daily routine.

We can travel on pennies a day or thousands of dollars. We can stay in a mud hut or a five-star luxury suite. We can travel as an independent traveler or on a package tour. Regardless of the style, destination, or length of our travels, we must seize the full spectrum of travel's endless possibilities.

In the course of my numerous wanderings, I have seen how travel has informed and empowered my life as well as the lives of my fellow travelers. I have witnessed the nature and extent of travel's positive power, the magnitude of its enriching and healing capabilities. Beyond its refreshing and revitalizing qualities, travel has the unmatched capacity to be a wellspring of self-discovery and personal growth, a path to ourselves.

While travel is replete with fun and adventure, travel also teaches directly, by reality, and often it is this reality which provides us with tremendous insight, scope, and depth. Travel

affords us the occasion to look both outward and inward, to enlighten our mind and transform our soul.

The Power of Travel is intended as a handy, concise, and easily accessible fountain of encouragement, motivation, and affirmation for all travelers and would-be travelers. Its pages are devoted exclusively to articulating and harnessing the full breadth of travel's potential within the context of our own personal and distinctive collection of individual travel experiences. The reflections, ruminations, and revelations contained in this everyday source are designed to

- inspire, nurture, and support you in all of your travel dreams and aspirations;

- offer you a greater and deeper connection with travel's expansive potential; and

- accompany you across travel's boundless landscapes of enrichment, healing, and personal growth.

Whether you are contemplating a journey or a jaunt, already on the road, or restlessly awaiting the next chapter in your travels, I hope that this book will take you where you need to go, sustain you in your path, and celebrate what you have experienced.

Read it in one trip. Or visit and revisit favorite passages as desired. Wander freely. Savor its landscape, on your own schedule, at home or along the way.

Before we set out, I would like to comment on certain aspects of my approach in the writing of this book.

▸ As you will note in the pages that follow, I use the pronoun "we." I do so because we are not alone in our experience of travel.

As travelers, we may be likened to a nation, a tremendous moving state, an extensive community with a set of similar experiences. We are at the forefront of humanity's push towards the frontier. Although the details of our individual travels may differ, we share the common bond of travel's powers.

▸ While I have incorporated selected quotations from a wide realm of notable individuals, what accompanies each quote is not meant as a direct interpretation of its original meaning or intention. Rather, I draw on each thoughtful reference solely as a spark for reflection, reset in an often new and different context.

▸ In turn, each reflection is intended merely as a rough map, broad and invit-

ing in its vision, allowing you to access and ruminate on your own unique experience of travel's enriching wonders.

▸ Woven through the book are various illustrations. We can think of these familar images as points of connection, and in between—on the page, in our minds, and across the miles—lies the magic of travel's powers.

▸ We have the ability to connect and reconnect with the full range of travel's powers regardless of whether our travels are short- or long-term, close to home or in some distant land. At times, I may seem to be addressing one scenario or the other, but I am not. Travel's potential translates across these differing paths. What's important is that we remain open and attuned to our varied travel experiences, ready to engage each of their many unfolding virtues.

Travel is and will continue to be a powerful but precious gift. Whether our travels are international, national, or local, we must continue to take responsibility for the gift of travel. As worldwide travel increases, so do the pressures on both our physical and our cultural environments.

Continue to respect our world, its people, its places, its animals, its landscape. Continue to respect nature. Continue to respect our differences. We owe that to ourselves, to each other, and to the generations yet to be.

Whether we're traveling to the farthest corners of the earth or to the next village, whether we're going for a couple of days or a year, the power of travel awaits. Make the time. Make the space. Live the power of travel.

Impulse

The Magic of Motion

From the very beginning of our creation, we are continuously moving, traveling. The journey of conception. Birth's journey. We enter this world, and we remain in constant motion. Even when we're not moving, we're moving. Moving through life, the journey of life.

Motion is a natural life force, a basic human instinct. We need to move, to explore, to satisfy our curiosity. We require the stimulation and inspiration offered by movement, by travel. Wanderlust is part of our basic humanity. We do not shun it or doubt its intentions.

We acknowledge our need for motion, for a change of scenery, faces, and places. We feel our motion. We welcome our motion. We embrace our motion—the magnificent thrust onward and away. We embrace the motion of our humanity.

Movement Is History

The history of humanity is a history of movement—remarkable, exceptional movement. Moses, Buddha, Mohammed, Jesus. Marco Polo, Christopher Columbus, Lao Tzu. Amelia Earhart, Jack Kerouac, Lawrence of Arabia. They all were travelers. Our collective history is one of eminent journeys.

Rooted in trust, hope, and faith, they pursued their beliefs, their certainties, their being. They moved forward in the direction of their convictions, into history—the history of travel, the history of humanity, our history. We move towards our place in history.

We think of those who have traveled before us, on our path. We begin to understand the history of our travels, movement over time. We understand our place in movement's path.

We Travel In Our Mind

We nurture our travel aspirations from childhood. Mysterious and enchanting faraway places capture our essence, create our longings. The templates of our travels rest deep in our needs, in our desires, in our soul. Somewhere unknown, as yet unseen, undiscovered. Geography unexplored, cultures unexperienced. The allure of There.

We journey in our head and in our heart. Our imagination fills in the missing pieces of information to complete our mind's voyage. We daydream, mental passports in hand, wandering off to magical places with magical names.

The Serengeti, Tibet, the Amazon. The Grand Canyon, Machu Picchu, Hollywood. The Galapagos, Angkor Wat, Istanbul. Havana, the Golden Triangle, Timbuktu.

Notions of beauty, calm, intrigue, romance. A white sandy beach; palm trees; and

17

warm, tranquil air. A peaceful rock garden in Kyoto. The hill tribes in Chang Mai. A cozy Parisian café. Images and fantasies stirring and growing, awaiting the light of real encounter.

Have we remained true to our travel dreams? Have we explored the furthest reaches of our traveler's soul?

We Heed Our
Travel Dreams

We sail out towards the horizon, and yet our feet remain firmly planted. Our imaginations are ripe with peregrinations to places we may or may never get to, just around the corner or in lands far away. Out of our mental transport germinate the seeds of our actualized journeys. We cradle and protect our cerebral crossings.

Where would we travel for an afternoon or a weekend? A week or a month? Six months or a year?

We cannot ignore our travel dreams. They are the rough sketches of what we will be, where we will go, what we will see, what we will truly experience. They are the makeshift signposts of who we will be, out there, in the world. The blueprints of our soul.

Why Travel

We travel to escape boredom. To explore. To rest. To attain balance. To understand other cultures. To seek adventure. To reflect. To gain perspective. To find romance and love. To conduct a religious or spiritual pilgrimage. To verify or experience things firsthand. To enrich ourselves.

We travel to pass through time and history. To discover our roots. To heal. To find peace and serenity. To test our limits. To do something original. To visit historic and cultural places of interest. To meet people. To conduct business. To learn another language. To work in another country. To volunteer our work. To get away from work.

We travel to relax. To have fun. To shop. To study. To be in motion. To feel a sense of direction. To climb a mountain. To discover ourselves. To search for a greater spirituality and purpose. To look for answers to life's bigger questions. To find home.

We travel because it's been three years since we took a week off. We travel because it's just a short distance away. We travel because it's something we promised ourselves a long time ago. We travel because it's time again. We travel because we are restless. We travel because we can. We travel because we must.

We connect with the reasons for our travels.

Life is either a daring adventure or nothing.
Helen Keller

Who We Are, and Who We Need to Be

We travel for other, less "socially acceptable" reasons. To avoid a decision. To avoid responsibility. To avoid a commitment. To look for a distraction, a diversion.

Whatever our motivation, we listen to our voice, that something we must do, our natural impulse. The urge to go. The desire to move, to reach out, to push our limits, to press beyond the known. To go somewhere, anywhere. Wherever we need to go. To take the time. For however long we need to go. To do what we need to do, now.

We Allow
Ourselves to Change
the Why

Our reasons for going may shift. Our *why* may end up to be something entirely different from what it was when we started. We may even lose sight of the *why* and not care if we ever find it again. It may not matter *why*. There may not be a *why*. The *why* may follow, or it may not. In fact, we may never really understand the *why* we thought we had.

Instead, we close our eyes, breathe in deeply, and feel the sheer power of our physical desire to go, to be somewhere fresh and inviting. We focus on that magnificent sensation. We stay there, in that place.

Our *why* evolves as we head forth into the wilderness of the unknown. We understand this change and receive it with grace.

The Power to
Just Go

The spirit and driving energy of travel empower us to make the jump, to leap. Just go. We have the power to realize our dreams, to push our limitations, to explore our most basic of urges. Just go. We have the power to embark, to head out, for one day, one week, or one year. Just go. We have the power to enrich ourselves with the beautiful, the adventurous, the fresh, the boldness of waking up to a new environment. Just go.

Travel's opportunity! Just go. When it knocks, we have the power to answer. Invite it in. Just go.

Response

Feeding Our Travel Bug

We read travelogues, magazines, and guide-books. We meet with travel agents, speak with friends, chat with travelers. We go to the library, delve through bookstores, surf the Internet. We check things out.

We ask. We listen. We stoke our curiosity and nourish our imagination. We kindle our journey. We set the event, absorb its dimension. We ease ourselves into travel's wonders and mysteries. We anticipate its delights. We sample its splendors.

Converting Dreams into Action

The replacement of desire with motion is bold and powerful. Daring and resolution are essential to realizing a dream.

What is the value of travel? What is the value of life and its experiences but to do that which is inside of us to do? We are obliged to pursue our greatest desires, our highest potential. We are resolved to do that which is inside of us to do.

Travel lets us live our dreams. Travel is witness to our courage to turn dreams into reality, to do anything we want to do. Travel attests to the strength of our will, our determination to push the boundaries of our spirit. Travel is the lifeline to our inner passion, to the life that lies within us all. Travel is the lifeline to our power.

Listening, to Ourselves

We tend to our traveler's soul. Dreams and visions of what may be. Yearnings for what may come to pass. We no longer ignore the voice of motion within. We no longer suppress our travel dreams. We listen to our traveler's soul.

We pay attention to ourselves, to Us. We do what our being demands, what our traveling Us desires.

We create a oneness with our traveling spirit, an agreement with our wanderlust—the chance to radiate its magical energy. Its time in the spotlight, life's spotlight. Its time to guide us through a day, a week, a month, a year. Our imagination is our beacon, the power of travel our star.

We honor our traveler's soul.

We Answer the Call of Our Wanderlust

We recognize the source of our misdirected, accumulating, unreleased energy. Our anxiety, tension, hesitation. We know how we feel when we need to get away and we can't, or we don't.

We acknowledge travel's ability to release our stored-up, pent-up energy—to channel our motion energy. We acknowledge how good we feel when we do get away, when we jump in that car, take off in that plane, kick back on that train.

Properly directed through motion, we give Us what we need, what we crave, what the sedentary life cannot do, what the non-traveling life cannot give.

Travel answers our requirement for motion. Purely, simply, directly. To move, to travel, to be.

Embracing Go

We let go of our reasons not to go. Money. Family. Work. Career. Obligations and responsibilities. We can't get away. No time. Keeping us from our dreams. From ourselves. From Us.

We think of the reasons we have created for not going. We write down each reason, every last one. Then we erase each reason, one by one, until the page is blank. No more excuses.

We rise to our travel needs, our outer journeys and inner quests, our reasons to go. We embrace our travels with passion and zeal.

We Go Now

We are not here forever. We have eternity to be still, but precious few years to experience the extent of our motion. We look honestly at what it is that we want out of life. We do what we want to do now. We go where we want to go now. We go where we need to go now. Regret is crippling. We go now.

We allow ourselves the freedom to take the time to go where our free minds and spirits will take us. Time is our most precious resource. We make the time for travel now. We carve it out if we need to. And we do need to. We go now.

We picture ourselves at the very end of life, on our last day alive. We take a really close and careful look at ourselves in that place, in that time. We look around at the room, the bed, the ceiling. We will be there one day. We connect to that image and hold it in our mind.

Where would we like to have gone but didn't go? What country or culture did we want to explore but never got the chance or availed ourselves of the opportunity? We go there, now. We go now.

Go

Our Journey Starts with Yes

We fix the date. We mark it on our calendar, make a reservation, buy our ticket. We know when we're going. A promise is kept.

From the very instant we decide to go, we are released. We feel the power of our decision, the surge of clarity. The power of our clarity. The strength of our commitment. We sense the power of travel's impending presence. Our mind is adrift, eagerly awaiting our physical departure.

We Prepare
Our Go

Each in our own way.

We plan. We overplan. We discuss. We overdiscuss. We research. We overresearch. We reserve our hotels. We double book, just in case. Each in our own way.

We shop. We read. We get our shots. We shop some more. We read some more. We get more shots. We get our passports. We get our visas. We pick up our tickets. We shop some more. We get our last set of shots. We wait impatiently with each passing day. Each in our own way.

We pack and repack. And repack. Each in our own way.

We don't speak to a soul. We don't read a thing. We don't make any reservations at all. We toss what we have into a bag and just go. Each in our own way.

We Carry What We Need

We take the essentials. And the nonessentials. Toiletries and cameras. Camping gear and hair dryers. A bottle of soap bubbles for the kids we meet along the way. Practical clothes, adventure clothes, fancy clothes. Mounds of maps. Essentials for some. Nonessentials for others.

We take what we need, what we require. For our freedom. Our own version of simplicity and balance. For us. It's our vacation, our trip, our overseas journey. A couple of trunks. A suitcase or two. A backpack. A daypack. A shoulder pack. A fanny pack. One solitary journal.

We know what we need. If we are wrong, we will know that too, in time, in our own way. We do lighten our burden, from our perspective, from our own individual and unique perspective. We understand what we need to make us happy, and we go.

Go *Is Before Us*

The pull towards our impending separation intensifies. Time narrows. Our anticipation thrusts us on board.

We are attuned to any passing travel reference. A travel tip. A sliver of history. Something on the news. Anything that may relate, in any way, to places we are going. Our travel antennae are up. We're at the gate. We see our path. We feel the power.

Right in front of us. Chosen. Taken. Possessed. Attained. We are empowered by the imminency of our crossing.

Departure

Life is sustained by movement, not by a foundation.
Antoine de Saint-Exupéry

We awaken on that morning of our farewell, on that day of our motion, forward, to places already been or never trodden. We are unstoppable. We surge forth, arms open wide. We leave with joy and love for those we leave behind, for those we have yet to meet, for points unacquainted but soon to be, for our homes away from Home.

Airport, bus terminal, train station. The check-in counter. "Tickets, please." Off with our luggage. "Enjoy your trip."

We say our good-byes. Smiles and tears, passions and fears. Customs and passport control. One last good-bye. One last wave. One last glance as we pass through security and into the unknown.

We Are Our Own Hero

Setting out makes us a hero to ourselves, for ourselves. For stepping out, for seizing our travel opportunities. For seizing life's opportunities.

For taking that first step. For getting in our car. For boarding that bus, that train, that ship, that plane. For releasing the ties of Home and crossing into another way, into another world, our world.

Movement, Glorious Movement

I travel not to go anywhere, but to go. I travel for travel's sake. The great affair is to move.

Robert Louis Stevenson

We fly. We taxi. We bus. We drive. We bike. We hike. We sail. We kayak. We canoe. We cruise. We hitch. We off-road. We take a "tuk-tuk." We jaunt. We journey. We move.

We sit back and feel motion. Motion *feels* good. Motion *feels* great. Motion centers our mental being. Motion sets out our perspective, the perspective we require to get where we're going. Motion separates us and draws us closer, simultaneously towards others and towards ourselves. Movement moves us from us and towards Us.

We relax into the rhythm of motion. Forward, forward, onward, onward. We move ahead. We pass over. We pass through. We pass by. From. Towards. We embody the tranquillity, excitement, and anticipation that is motion, that is travel.

Welcome Motion

We surrender to the linear direction of forward movement. Towards some enchanting frontier. Watching what is become what was and fade into the horizon, out of sight and out of mind.

Motion relegates the noise to that which was and leaves us to what will be, to the rising whispers of what will be, to the magic ahead in the motion of life. We embrace the transition of our mobility.

We feel the anxiety, the stress, the built-up energy dissipate. Gradually. And gratefully. Gracefully. We let it all go. We breathe in, deeply, and feel the motion. We revel in release. The joyous release of everything. The joyous release of motion.

Leaving Our Weight Behind

We rise. We rise above ourselves, above our worries, above our obsessions, the obsessions of the everyday. Above the compulsions of habit. Above our responsibilities, duties, obligations—imagined or real. We float away from us and towards Us. Towards our other selves, towards others.

Familiarity's burden lifts. Heaviness drains. We begin to soar. Gestures of a new lightness take shape. We welcome travel's compelling freshness, its robust touch.

We bid good riddance to the burden, the stress and the strain. We treasure our new levity. We savor the buoyancy of our soul.

We Deserve Our Travels

We work towards our path, to live our journey, our unique journey. We acknowledge our desire to reap the wonders of travel, to receive its many gifts, to unfold travel's multicolored quilt.

We warrant travel's ecstasy, its astounding presence in our lives, its bountiful rewards. We do not second-guess its offer. We accept its deliverance. We merit its lush and powerful joy. We hold its dynamic potential. We treat ourselves to its way.

Freedom

Our Own Path

We set the path. We set the path by following the impulse. We follow our own impulse. We go where we must go. We have limitless routes, all of which take us where we're going. Each is original to us, at that particular moment in time. In that instant.

We go back to places we've been, and try to retrace our steps, only to find that a new avenue eagerly awaits us, different from the last. Another individual road. Each of our travel experiences represents a unique set of encounters with people, places, and events which never can be duplicated, only cherished.

Our tracks bear the joys and revelations of our unparalleled journals, the journals of our unparalleled course. We rejoice in our authentic passage.

Travel Is Individual

We all have different needs, demands, requirements, comforts.

We travel solo, or with friends. We join groups. We roam from place to place. We stay in a favorite city or village, and travel from there. We live in luxury, or on a shoestring. We have a strict timetable and travel plan, or we prefer a more relaxed, easygoing itinerary. We insist on no schedules at all.

Travel is inclusive. Regardless of our philosophy of travel, we are all travelers, whatever we may call ourselves. Adventure Traveler. Tourist. Holiday maker. Luxury Tourist. Backpacker. Globetrotter. Overlander. We are all travelers. Regardless of how we travel, travel is powerful. For all, travel is heroic.

In the Moment

We are not burdened by the details and concerns of anchored life. We can just be. In the present.

We hover, weightless, like the breeze, in the immediacy of the instant, in the now of our lives. So much is new, unfamiliar, undiscovered. Our mind is occupied with what is right before it. No overthought. No "other" thought. No need to look for things to think of, to take us out of the moment. We focus on the moment.

We are intensely aware of the moment. We live the moment. Uncluttered, we are free to absorb, crisply and clearly. We are Here. We are here because we are here. Now. Living now.

In my everyday life, I would often feel a stifling awareness of the purpose behind everything I did. Every book I read, every movie I saw, everything had to have a reason behind it. From time to time, I felt the urge to do something for no reason at all.

Michael Crichton

Release

We unleash ourselves into the world. We unleash our Selves into the world.

We set forth towards our desires, towards what we are. Released to the world, our original dreams take on new life, new energy. We dream new dreams of places and people yet to come, of experiences yet to be. We are alive.

We expand our dreams. A kayak trip through the Queen Charlottes. A climb up Kilimanjaro. A stroll on the Great Wall of China. A road trip across America. Why not?

New ventures. New quests. New aspirations. New inspirations. We release and do. We release and truly be. We see the vast potential of what is before us. We block nothing.

Independence

**Happiness is when
what you think,
what you say, and
what you do are
in harmony.**
Mahatma Gandhi

Our spirits are free. Free to roam, to wander, to explore, to examine, to discover, to enjoy, to love, to flourish. Free to enjoy the latitude of chance, the scope of the unknown. A license to unshackle our mind, unchain our desire, unfurl the tapestry of our imaginative being. We are our autonomous selves, sailing with travel's empowering winds.

Roam. Wander. Explore. Examine. Discover. Enjoy. Love. Flourish.

Follow the Impulse

We're not bound by rules. We do as we wish, according to a plan or on a whim, on a moment's thought or none at all. We go when and where we want to go. We follow our fancy, our own inclination, our own liberating process. We follow the impulse.

At every turn, we respond as we wish, in that instant, in that emancipating moment. Naturally. Instinctively, as children. From the center of our spontaneous being. We follow the impulse.

We come to trust our impulsive voice. Where we should go. Whom we should trust. What we should do. We come to trust our impulsive, knowing Self. We follow our impulse.

Choice

Afoot and light-hearted I take to the open road,

Healthy, free, the world before me,

The long brown path before me leading wherever I choose.
Walt Whitman

What to see. What to eat. Where to stay. Where to go. How to go. When to go. When to stop. Who to meet. What to listen to. What to do. When to do it. How to do it. How to be.

The freedom to go as we wish. The freedom to follow our flow. The freedom to go with the flow of others. The choice is ours. How, when, why, where, what, who. We are blessed with the decisions of travel.

We think of our best travel choices. Our worst. And what we learned along the way.

Anywhere and Everywhere

We travel in our own country. We travel in our parents' country. We travel where we've been, where we've never been, where we've always wanted to go.

We travel where we've heard is great, not to be missed. A "must-see." We travel where the tour is going, from where they just came. We travel where they didn't go, where they wouldn't go. We travel where only we would go.

We travel where the next ride is heading, where the dhow is sailing. We travel where the winds of Chance take us.

We travel towards our possibilities. We travel towards our potentialities. Anywhere and everywhere, we travel towards our dreams and ourselves.

We Go to Us

We leave the everyday. We leave the common for the sacred. To the sacred.

We need to go where we are most deeply touched. Most deeply moved. Most deeply stimulated. Most richly Us. We go to the Divine. We go where we are at ease, relaxed, at peace.

The ocean. The forest. The desert. The mountains. The country. The city. The Gulf of Mexico. The Redwoods. The Sahara. The Alps. Tuscany. Rio. We go where we are intrigued, inspired, in awe.

We encounter our sacred Self. We touch our sacred Self. We respect our dreams. We respect our hearts. Our dreams open our hearts. Our dreams reveal our divine. Our divine reveals our Self, our free and sacred Self. We go where we are most our sacred Self.

Spontaneity

> When you come to a fork in the road, take it.
> Yogi Berra

Just like that. Our day tour cancels at the last minute. What to do? Just like that. Our car breaks down in some quaint hamlet. What to do? Just like that.

We meet a new friend who insists we join him or her for dinner. We go. Just like that. We explore a colorful market while waiting for our next bus or train. We go. Just like that.

We look for opportunities for spontaneity. We anticipate opportunities for spontaneity. We *create* opportunities for spontaneity. We leave an hour each day without any plans. A whole day. For some, a whole week, a whole month. Rootless, groundless, minute-by-minute spontaneity. We indulge in our spontaneity. We swim confidently in our spontaneity. Just like that.

Travel Is Ageless

When I was very young and the urge to be someplace was on me, I was assured by mature people that maturity would cure this itch. When years described me as mature, the remedy prescribed was middle age. In middle age I was assured that greater age would calm my fever and now that I am fifty-eight perhaps senility will do the job. Nothing has worked.

John Steinbeck

Age is irrelevant to the fact of departure. Whether we're eighteen or eighty-one, we are able to travel and reap the rewards of our journey. Our mind goes, and our body follows. Only the perspective changes.

Travel at twenty, and do the same trip at forty or sixty. The fact of motion is resplendent in its nondiscrimination, open to all. We appreciate the time of our travel as much as our time of travel.

We compare how places have changed over the course of years, as we visit them at different points in our life. We wonder how places will change when we return after ten years, and then again after twenty. Mirrored reflections of ourselves.

Delight in Anonymity

Suddenly, at any given moment, on any given day, in any given place, we realize that nobody in the world knows where we are. Nobody. We're nameless, unknown. A mystery. An enigma.

We do not fear our anonymity. We extol its exhilarating and liberating qualities. We are comforted by its release. We savor its power, the power of its unleashing. We go forth in its energy, its open agenda. We are prepared for its potential. In that moment, we are whoever we want to be. We are who We are. A traveler. Free. Free to be.

S o a r

Travel lets us soar, frees our imagination to soar, to new altitudes, to new planes.

We soar beyond the original spark, beyond the root so firmly planted, beyond the limitations of our mind. We soar with all our senses. We soar with all that's new and unexpected, all the gifts of the unimagined. Infinite newness. Unlimited potential. Boundless soaring.

Discovery

Summoning Our Senses

Travel enriches what we see, what we smell, what we taste, what we hear. What we feel. Travel heightens our human experience. Everything about us seems tuned in to all that surrounds us. Travel enraptures our entire being.

Travel strikes with force at our powers of appreciation and joy, cracking open that which might otherwise go unnoticed, piercing our inner soul. We are infused with the exotic aroma of incense, the full magnitude of a bolt of lightning in a sudden summer thunderstorm, the perfect brightness of a full moon, the shrill peeping chime of crickets in the crisp night air, the scent of a pine forest after a spring rain. What we once overlooked is now everything we desire.

We see. We feel. We smell. We taste. We hear. We listen acutely, to our world. We must. We can't not. We are open. Intensely open, intensely aware.

The Magnificence
of the New

Fresh landscapes, fresh people. Fresh stimuli to invigorate our spirit, to wake us up. We are assaulted from all angles, at every corner, with every opportunity. We soak in dazzling new flavors. What awakens us most?

Our senses are like sponges, fully imbibing the richness of novel environments and the aura of original faces. We are preoccupied, decoding strange customs, unique ways. Discerning the familiar and exposing the brilliant luster of the newly discovered, the odd, the peculiar.

We process everything. Reveling in the new. Reveling in the novel. Reveling in the freshness. We are excited. We inhale deeply and passionately, absorbing the new straight back into our essence. We are fully awake.

Time Changes

Packed with experience, our travel days seem to expand. Life is larger, teeming. Movement distorts time to our advantage. We lose sight of time. Each moment of travel connects to the next. Each moment is saturated, brimming, filled to capacity.

We slow down and absorb life, capture and understand life. The sense of where we are heading and why. We take the time to discover time. We maximize each day. Each second is alive, each moment bursting. The hours and minutes swell to meet our needs, to accommodate our dreams, to optimize each second of our journey.

On the Wings of Serendipity

Travel surprises us. We bump into people we haven't seen in years, childhood friends. We meet the famous and the infamous. A turn down the next street, right instead of left, and a new friend is created, a friend for life. Left instead of right, and we rediscover the charming little restaurant we'd visited years before and long forgotten. Stay at this place instead of that, and suddenly we're traveling north instead of south, east instead of west.

No matter our intended design or schedule, Chance is our ever-present travel partner in discovery. Fate and Destiny orchestrate our journey, map out our path. Fortune and Luck plot our course, serve as our compass. We applaud the happenstance of our ways, our happy accidents, our little miracles. We recognize and celebrate the Kismet in our travels, the synchronistic signposts of our soul.

Travel Is Naïve and Wondrous

Travel reminds us of all there is to learn and understand. There is no limit to what travel may teach us, what experience may show us, what the world may reveal to us. We realize that we only think we know. But we don't.

As we are not *part of* our shifting environment, our understanding remains limited, cursory. Humbled. We pick up little bits and pieces along the way, morsels of insight, not enough to wholly light our path but sufficient to guide us, step by step, glimpse by glimpse. Precious specks of light that lead us forth on travel's journey.

We Explore

Like a child, we venture freely without inhibition. Like a child, we improvise our way through an unexperienced world. We are presented with opportunity, and travel gives us permission to explore, like a child.

Away from Home, there is so much we don't understand. So much we need to understand. So much we want to understand, explore, examine. We must understand. We must explore. We must examine.

Once away, we are less restrained. We don't withhold. We pursue our curiosity, freely and openly. We take the time to be curious. We take the time to probe. We let go of tried and true ways. We take the time to improvise, to sample, to taste.

Outward and Inward

We scurry up a massive learning curve. Everything is inviting. We strive to make sense of all that's out there. As much as we can, we struggle to participate in what's before us. We act and react. We ask and listen. We learn about the people we meet and the places we visit. Ultimately, we learn about ourselves.

We question ourselves. We revisit ourselves. We look inward. We look outward into a mirror. We ask ourselves important questions. We question what we are seeing, what we are witnessing. We examine our assumptions, how our beliefs are being challenged. We may not find answers, but we search. We search and question. And go forth in our journey, the journey of our inner landscape.

We Rediscover

Travel offers us the opportunity to rediscover. To rediscover fun, beauty, joy. To rediscover compassion, friendship, loyalty. To rediscover adventure, pursuit, excellence. To rediscover forgiveness, acceptance, surrender. To rediscover solitude, stillness, tranquillity. To rediscover walking, dancing, jumping. To rediscover dining, sipping, conversing.

What would we like to rediscover in our travels? What have we already rediscovered?

We rediscover health, strength, power. We rediscover perspective, vision, clarity. We rediscover simplicity, freedom, purity of the human spirit.

Encounter

People

People traveling from here to there, somewhere to somewhere. People there at our departure . . . good-bye. People there at our arrival . . . hello.

People on the plane, on the ship, on the train, on the bus, in our shared taxi. On the road.

Doing what people do when they travel. Preparing dinner in the kitchen at our hostel. Eating fresh-baked bread at the table next to us in our cozy bed and breakfast. Pitching tent at the next campsite. Sipping afternoon cocktails at the bar in our hotel.

People at home, the visited. People living, simply living, as we pass through. Hawking, eating, drinking, laughing, living, dying. Greeting, inviting, welcoming, preparing, opening up their lives to the traveler. Conversing, engaging, getting to know people. Different lan-

guages. Different dialects. Different accents. Understanding other people.

We recall the people we have met while traveling. Where we met. How we met. What they said. What we said. Encounter.

Chance meetings with people. Locals. Foreigners. Moving in the direction of other travelers, other people. Stopping and talking. Walking and talking. Eating and talking. Drinking and talking. Traveling and talking. Traveling and communicating. Traveling and smiling. Traveling and knowing. Travel is people.

Children

Kids. And more kids. Innocent. And not so innocent. But cute. Disarming kids. Curious and engaging.

They find us. They search us out. They run towards us. Brothers, sisters, and friends in tow. Strangers. Little strangers.

Our eyes connect. Their smiles draw us in. Some cautious. Some direct. Very direct. Like kids. Clean-cut and well dressed. Snotty-nosed and tattered. Minimagnets in our journey.

We play a game. We teach our language, a word or two. They teach us theirs. My name is. Your name is. I am from. You are from. They sing a song. A tune they learned in school. We sing together.

They touch our hair on our head, on our arms, on our legs. We take their pictures. We take one together. They want copies. Addresses scrawled on tiny shreds of paper.

Our fellow explorers. Moments of shared connection and discovery. Powerful flickers of openness and hope.

What do we share with the children we meet? A story. A song. A smile. A simple hug. A sacred moment.

We Have Permission to Be a Stranger

We are all pretty much alike when we get out of town.
Kim Hubbard

We are a stranger to each other, to our fellow travelers. We are a stranger to the visited. We float in a myriad of different cultures. We're often misunderstood. We don't have to know everything. We don't have to be familiar with everything. We may try, but we're not obliged to figure everything out.

We are naive. We are charming. We are intriguing. We're forgiven for our mistakes, our misinterpretations, our exotic ways. And we respect.

We notice when being a stranger has helped. We remember when it has been most challenging. We welcome the chance to be a stranger.

Hospitality

> [The traveler] will discover, how many truly kind-hearted people there are, with whom he never before had, or ever again will have any further communication, who yet are ready to offer him the most disinterested assistance.
> Charles Darwin

Somebody gives us directions. Advice. A friendly suggestion. A local tip. A safe ride back to our hotel. A helping hand.

Someone invites us into their home. A warm meal. A roof over our heads. Somebody cares. Generosity. Beneficence.

We are greeted. We are received. We are made to feel welcome. We are trusted and accepted. We learn to trust and accept.

Whose hospitality have we never forgotten? How can we show our appreciation? How can we reciprocate?

Merci. Shukran. Eskerrik asko. Dekuji. Dank. Dankan. Kiitos. Danke. Euxaristɷ. Dhan-ya-vaad. Tochia. Terima kasih. Grazie. Arigato. Gamsa-hamnida. Xìe xìe. Tack. Maururu. Agyamanac. Salamat. Dziekuje. Obrigada. Spasibo. Hvala. Blago darya. Dankie. Köszönöm. Gracias. Ahsante sana. Todah rabah. Khawp khun krup. Sagol. Shakria. Thank you.

Conversation

We chat with those we've just met. Going to, coming from. About where we've been. Where we're going. Where we are. Who we are. Who they are. Who we say we are. Who they say they are. Who we think we are.

Secrets and truths we would never tell anybody, except now, in that moment. To a stranger, in the seat next to us, across the dinner table, in their home, on our path.

Questions. Answers. More questions. The little questions. The big questions. Questions of direction.

We indulge in long-winded discourses about nothing, about everything. Everything imaginable, open for discussion. The bold exchange of transience. Uninhibited, candid, upfront. Divulging. Entrusting. Free to ask, free to answer. Free to agree, free to disagree. The dialogue of travel.

Friendship

We relish the constant opportunity for encounter. We're open to meeting new people, new friends. We're prepared for instantaneous friendships. Relationships based on possibilities rather than probabilities.

We know our time together may be brief, even momentary. A few minutes, an hour, a day. We value the time we do spend together. We invest our passion in those we have a genuine interest in getting to know. We spill our guts. We listen attentively. We're acutely aware of the fleeting but intense nature of our comradeship.

Our new friends are locals, curious, like us. Our new friends are our fellow travelers, temporarily on the same route, in the same space, like us. We share a commonality that rises above our countries of origin, above the medley of language and cultural barriers. Our motives seem purer on the road, friendship for the sake of friendship. Faith in friendship.

We think of a friend we never would have met if we had not traveled. There, in that place, at that time. How much richer is our life for that friendship? We recall when the two of us first met. Did we know immediately that we'd be friends? Could we have formed a friendship if we had met at home? We are grateful for our traveling friendships.

We Return to Our New Friends

We bump into people we've met earlier in our travels. We have a drink. We grab a bite to eat. We catch up. We bandy tales of our travels. We trade suggestions about where to go, where to stay, and how to get there. We swap humorous anecdotes. We laugh. And we laugh some more.

We revisit the visited. We have a drink. We grab a bite to eat. We catch up. We tell tales of our travels. They tell us of change or no change. We laugh. And we laugh some more.

We say good-bye . . . until our next meeting. Until we exchange letters, pictures. Until we talk on the phone. Until we visit each other again as nontravelers, as friends. We toast our friendship, the friendship of our ways.

A Gift to Ourselves and Others

We share the spirit and joy of our journey with those we meet. We let others be affected by us. We influence them. They influence us. We learn from them, about them. They learn from us, about us. We open up to others. We interact openly, freely.

We forge the course with our fellow travelers. We cut a path with the visited, diamonds along our traveler's trail, precious jewels shining brilliantly in unfamiliar territory. We share gestures, observations, tales, laughter. We share the abundance of our travels. They share the abundance of place. There is plenty for everyone.

Our time together is all too brief, ephemeral. We promise to keep in touch. We hope we will. We swap telephone numbers, e-mail addresses. We exchange gifts, our love and friendship, keepsakes of this juncture in

our journey. We exchange the best of ourselves, our dreams. We are grateful for the precious gift of travel.

We bid each other good-bye and look back, pausing to absorb the moment, to capture it in our soul. What gift from within do we leave behind in the souls of those we meet? What gift from within do we leave behind in the souls of those we touch?

Travel Brings Us to Nature

And nature to us. Close to Us. Face to face. Limb to limb.

Amazonian rain forests. Solitary quiver trees in the Kalahari. Passing icebergs off the coast of Greenland. Windswept dunes on the Baltic.

Hippos bathing in the Okavango Delta. Kangaroos pronking in the Australian Outback. A moose chomping on a lily pad in the morning mist of a Canadian lake.

Balmy breezes. Drenching humidity. Monsoons. Typhoons. The wettest of wet. Crisp Arctic air. Howling, pounding wind. Creeping mountain clouds. Scorching desert sun.

We travel through nature. We travel with nature. We discover nature in its power, in its magnificence. In its brilliant, radiant message. In all of its rich and wild glory. We are overwhelmed in its presence. We are blissfully overjoyed.

We Capture Our Unique Encounters

An extraordinary skyline. A lioness and her cubs. A perfect sunrise. A not-to-be-forgotten sunset. Eternal.

The two of us. The group of us. Just me. Against the picturesque. In the market. With the falls in the background. Standing proudly at the summit. In front of the fountain where we met. The shot. Conclusive proof we were there. Eternal.

Them. The visited. The observed. At home. At work. Bathing in the river. Selling bananas from a stall. Triumphant in a game of soccer. Living their lives. As we see it. As we capture it. As we remember it. The power of our eyes, the motion of our hands. Eternal.

On film. On video. In our journals. In our writings. Carefully written missives from abroad. Hastily scrawled postcards from days and weeks gone by. Cybermail from right now. Eternal.

We commit our experiences to memory. In our thoughts, in our hearts. The records, sketches, and chronicles of our travels. Definitive, fleeting moments of our moving soul. Eternal.

We Are Nature's Witness

We encounter the power of nature, its awe-some abundance and diversity. We experience its majesty, its splendor. Its enormity, scope, height, depth, expanse. Its hold on time. Its permanence. And impermanence. Bastion of the secrets of time.

We behold nature's hospitality, its simple nurturing. Providing us with what we need. The shade of its splendid branches. A warm fire. A cave in which to spend the night. Clear spring water. Fresh fish. We celebrate what we have. Plenty. Nature's caring hands. Travel's watchful eye.

Nature stops us, obliges us to think, to ponder, to appreciate its inviting display. Nature forces us to acknowledge, value, love, treasure. Someone else's environment, someone else's landscape, someone else's garden. Someone else's grand backyard. Our environment, our landscape, our garden. Our grand backyard. Nature is gratitude.

Our Special Spots

A mountain peak. A hidden cove. A country lane. A chapel. A neighborhood bar. Little corners of the earth. Little corners of our earth. Our little corners. Our special spots.

Once just names in a guidebook, dots on a map, unknown destinations of intrigue. Now felt, touched, walked upon, imbued. Magical outposts of significance, highly personal significance, sanctioned by experience, embedded deep in our being. Elevated to Significant. Inscribed into our life's record, our life's log, our life's memoir.

Which unfamiliar dot on the map calls out to us? What draws us there? Where do we long to return? What draws us back?

Places which form our new reality, permanent places in our heart, eternal connections to our soul.

We Find
New Places to
Call Home

We have permission to stop, to reestablish a sense of place, membership in a settled community. Recognizable reference points in our condition of constant change. We answer our desire for stability.

We take breaks in our travels. A couple of days. A couple of weeks. A month. Six months. A whole year. We get a job, a different job. In a bar. Teaching English. Scuba diving. We study. We volunteer. We do what we've never done before, never thought we'd ever do.

We take the time to absorb, to take things in. Different environments, different languages, different cultures. We have our favorite places to shop, to eat, to drink, to relax, to meet other people. We use the same key, the same bed, our bed, for now.

What is it about our Home away from Home that makes us feel so at home?

We feel at ease. Part of. They recognize our faces. They call us by name. The details of their lives become ours. Friends for more than a day, more than a week. Home, for now. In our hearts, forever.

Joy

F u n

L ots of fun. Simple fun. Lots of simple fun. En-
tertaining, amusing, exhilarating fun. Recre-
ational, pleasureful, reveling fun. Deserving fun.

The unknown is fun. The unseen is fun.
The untried is fun. The unexpected is fun. The
unheard is fun.

We laugh. We giggle. We cry tears of laughter. We can't stop laughing. Things amuse us.
We amuse ourselves. We amuse others. Others
amuse us.

We frolic in our fun. Fanciful, frantic,
frenetic, festive, fantastical, frenzied, foolish,
forgiving, full-on, fabulously free, fly-by-the-
seat-of-our-pants, falling-down, foreign fun.

Food

Travel is definitely food. Mouthwatering, savory, luscious delectables from afar. Memorable meals.

Endless helpings of fresh pasta and countless glasses of homemade wine with family and friends in a small Italian village. Barbequed skewers on the side of the road in Lamu. Dim sum in Hong Kong. Cape Malay biboutie in South Africa. Crepes in Brittany. Banana pancakes in Uganda. Spicy smoked meat in Montreal. Yak butter tea with our Sherpa guide in the Himalayas.

Travel is spending an entire day feasting. Dining in some quaint little restaurant in the middle of nowhere. Being invited to somebody's house for a home-cooked meal, somebody we met just moments before. Gorging on a hotel's grand buffet. Grazing in the French countryside. Munching hot dogs over a campfire.

Reminiscences about the strangest food we've ever sampled, our most comforting meal, our most welcome repast. Recipes gathered from here and there, to savor when we're at home.

Grabbing that quick bite on the way to our next destination. Plane food. Train food. Cruise food. Truck stops. Eating that thing we shouldn't have eaten but we wanted to give it a try. Good or bad, travel is food.

Music

Translatable rhythms of our international language. Moving. Stirring. Celebrating.

A Bedouin playing his flute atop an ancient temple in Petra. Christmas mass in a small village in the Andes. The steady drone of monks chanting. A Broadway musical. Choir practice in St. Paul's Cathedral. Crickets at night. Buskers in the streets of Krakow.

Reinventing song lyrics around a campfire in Zanzibar. Three African sisters harmonizing hymns of Jesus in the light of a full moon. The strains of amateurs in a Tokyo karaoke bar.

Music to enhance the places we're visiting. Consoling. Reassuring. Comforting. Our own portable moods, Walkman moments, staring out the window of a jam-packed bus on our way to the next town. Or on deck, gazing out to sea.

We return with indigenous tunes, to carry us to places we've been, to satisfy our longings, to transport our soul.

Music of the road and for the road. Melodies that mend, mollify, and mesmerize. Rhythms that resonate and reverberate with time.

Adventure

Base camp. Sunrise at the summit of a dormant volcano. Last day of our twelve-day trek. The exhilarating seconds of free fall before the bungee snaps us skyward.

High-siding and then flipping on our last rapid. Trudging across an overflowing river, our backpacks balanced overhead. Watching nervously as our Basotho pony steps precipitously along a mountain ledge. Slip-sliding our way across the face of a cascading waterfall.

The Gruesome Twosome. The Big Five. Overlanding the African plain. Mountain biking the DMZ. Deep-sea diving off the coast of Cuba. Hot-air ballooning over the Namib desert.

We strive for that which most reenergizes our spirit. For that which best captures our passion. For that which pushes us the farthest towards Us, towards the outer reaches of our best Us.

Heightened adrenaline. Physical endurance. Mental challenge. Pushing, reaching, stretching us beyond our limits. Balance. Accomplishment. Joyful, breathtaking achievement.

R o m a n c e

Romantic notions of other places, of other people. Steeped in the unknown, the unseen, the unexperienced. Mystery, fantasy, excitement. Adventures of the loving kind.

Liaisons of love. On the road, in the air, on the sea. Titillating trysts of travel. Reckless rendezvous of amorous souls. Momentous affairs of the moment. Our special place. Our special restaurant. Our special room in that inn. Fantasies fulfilled. Entries in journals, glimpses and guessing. Where did we meet? Powerful and passing.

Legacies of love. Sustained passions. Rekindled through the trials of travel. Celebrations of devotion. Recaptured on crescent-mooned cruises, nights brimming with wine and freedom, an evening ride in a sultry Saigon cyclo. The enchanted, magical fullness of the traveling heart. Where did we meet? Powerful and lasting.

We Find Our Serenity

A much-needed breath in our travel day. A pause. A measure of calm in our sea of change. A temporary oasis. Peace.

Traveling sanctuaries. A quiet park bench. The coolness of the monastery's floor beneath our bare feet. Hymns and chants. The solemn silence of a cemetery. Peace.

Away from the traffic, the pulse of people. The noise fades. Refuges of respite and reflection. Havens and harbors. Shelters and retreats for our soul. Peace.

We Take Time-Out

We rest. We relax. Deep, satisfying rest. Renewal, revitalization. A clearing, a cleansing. We breathe deeply, fully.

Wandering aimlessly through a tiny village. Sleeping on the beach, easy and light. An entire day sipping coffee at a sidewalk café, watching others pass. Local life. Other travelers passing without us. An afternoon, a whole afternoon of nothing. Nothing at all.

When was our last time-out?

A few hours, a day, a week. A whole holiday of nothing at all but time-out. Awash in a sea of empty, stupendously lazy days and nights. Time to rebalance. Time to regenerate. Time to reflect. Time to retake ourselves. Delicious, uncompromising time-out.

Travel Is Rapture

Travel rewards us with peak experiences of intensity, zeal, and passion. Miraculous moments of eternity and ecstasy. Eruptions of abandon, release, surrender. Encounters that captivate, enthrall, and dazzle.

Events that mesmerize, hypnotize, enchant. Actions that astound, overwhelm, stagger. Accomplishments that empower. Memories that last lifetimes. Unique moments of splendor and joy, temptation and seduction, celebrations of our being.

Holding us to that second, that minute, that hour, that day in time, in our life, in our travels. Everlasting pinnacles in our soul.

Challenge

Rejoice in the Freedom of Our Uncertainty

We release ourselves from set routines, recognizable places, and predictable outcomes. We launch ourselves out of our own orbit and into unexplored worlds. Unexplored cities and villages. Unexplored forests and coastlines. Unexplored faces and tongues. Unexplored until now.

We set out to explore, to explore uncertainty and all of its surprises. We expect the unexpected. We wade through possibilities, enter open doors. On the other side—freedom.

Boundaries and limitations fall as we surge towards new frontiers. We are propelled towards freedom's frontier. Freedom's journey. We delight in freedom's uncertainty.

We Welcome the Untamed

We do not know the road ahead. We cannot know the road ahead. No matter how much we plan and arrange, or how well we organize and coordinate, we cannot envision what travel has in store for us.

We anticipate the uncontained. We appreciate that which is in our power, and we acknowledge that which is not. We let the ungoverned have its way. We don't resist the untamed. We receive its surprises. We laud its revelations. We honor its constant presence, its predictable unpredictability. We accept it as part of our experience and surrender to its reality. As travelers, we embrace its enlightenment, its rescue.

The Stake in
Our Dream

**Experience is one
thing you can't get
for nothing.**
Oscar Wilde

We prepare for the unexpected. And the un-expected happens, and we didn't expect it.
We tempt Chance, Fate, Fortune, Luck. We
cross over the line, our line of the safe and familiar. We venture out, hedging our bets, gambling
on our next step, the next road.

What is the riskiest thing we have done in
our travels? The most dangerous? The most
embarrassing? The riskiest thing we ever could
imagine doing?

We cross the boundaries of cultures, communication, custom, ritual. We misconstrue,
misunderstand, misperceive. We infer, specu-
late, conjecture. We seek credibility, acceptance.
We weigh the likelihoods, the possibilities, the
potentialities, the probabilities.

We learn, we grow, we thrive in the world
of hope and promise. We trust. We laugh. We
stand humbled. We accept the risk of our in-
vestment, the stake in our dream.

Adversity Is the Moment

Things go differently than we anticipated. Discomfort, loneliness, frustration, or even seeming catastrophe. Differently than anticipated, but not differently from what is meant to be. In that moment.

Sardine seating on a local bus. The bed's too hard. The bed's too saggy. I asked for a "soft sleeper" and got stuck with a "hard sleeper." There's no hot water. They shut off all the water. Our compartment is too crowded. The place is filthy. The place is too noisy. That damn mosquito wouldn't stop all night long. We miss our friends, our family.

Miscommunication. Missed departures and missed arrivals. Delayed flights. Train strikes. Canceled plans. Waiting. And more waiting. Desperately trying to catch some semblance of sleep as we await our next connection. It's colder than we thought. It's hotter than we thought. It's wetter than we thought. Diarrhea, dysentery, never-before-seen rashes. The host of different ailments of travel. Things that seem to happen only on the road.

Do we view adversity as a challenge, or as something to avoid when traveling? What has been our greatest test of physical adversity? Mental adversity? How did we deal with it then, in that traveling moment?

We want to be anywhere else but there. We think of things to console ourselves, to ease our pain, to ease our predicament. Our favorite food, our favorite people, our favorite place, our warmest piece of clothing. We think of things that are better. We think of things that are worse.

We remember why we're there. We eschew doubt. We shun misgivings. We focus on moving through. Adversity is our teacher. Adversity is the adventure. We look back and laugh. We embrace the odyssey that is each day, each moment of our traveling ways, each challenging moment.

Going Forward

Travel is finding solutions to problems we encounter and continuing ahead. The tribulations and hardships of the traveler. Moments that seem like steps backward are now recognized as steps toward.

We take a deep breath and play the cards, the cards of our journey. Our cards. We keep things in perspective. We focus on our present circumstances and go forth, grow forth. We maintain clarity of purpose, clarity of vision. Things are as they should be. We keep going. Outward.

We gather our strength, our confidence, our power. Perseverance. Tenacity. Determination. Onward. We revel in the challenge of our travels.

In the Heartland of Our Confidence

The more we travel, the more we travel. Experience the unfamiliar and it becomes familiar, understood. Experience displaces hesitation. Experience displaces fear. Caution yields to confidence. Faith and trust grow strong, filled with the power of travel.

Gone are our misgivings, our reservations, our qualms about travel. Gone are the apprehensions associated with going from what we know to what we have yet to know.

We are free to appreciate, untethered to our fears. Decisiveness abounds. We travel towards our fear, and with our fear. We are empowered by our own push to the frontier, the frontier of our fears, in the heartland of our confidence.

Travel Moves Us Through

Travel takes control away from us, exposing our weakest points. We are acutely aware of our vulnerability. We are naive, unaccustomed, unacquainted, unversed. We are ignorant, roaming in the darkness of the unfamiliar. We are lonely, lost, disoriented.

Travel pushes us across the chasm. We are moved to explore the mysterious, to confront our fear, to venture beyond the challenging, cryptic crevasses of our path.

Travel gives us control, revealing our strongest points. We are acutely aware of our invincibility. We are wise, well accustomed, well acquainted, well versed. We are knowing, marching in the light of the familiar. We are among friends and know exactly where we are.

Travel springs fountains of knowledge, insight, and strength. Travel empowers us by taking us on a critical human journey from fear and resistance to trust and surrender.

Insight

Live the Imagined

We travel, and suddenly places that once were mere fantasy acquire context, substance, presence. People, places, names, and numbers take on significance. Facts become relevant. Mere information ripens into experience and insight.

From the moment of our arrival, a reality sets in, the imagined takes on form. A new version of how things are. A reality we can attach to and hold. No longer imposed but organic. Arising out of our experiences, seeping into our being. Flushing into our world, filtered and unfiltered, pure and impure. Digested and then processed into something comprehensible, understood.

New places and people. Once imagined. Now here. Now in front of us. Now experienced. Now lived.

Treasure Our History

We absorb the sights. Tourist sights, travel sights, historical sights. We check them out, for ourselves. Places of interest. Places of significance. Museums. Gardens. Shrines. Churches. Monuments. Archaeological ruins.

What are we searching for on our historical quests? Which place most transports us to another time?

Crossroads of civilization. Relics of humanity. Relics of us. Preserving our triumphs and our tragedies. The best of humanity. The far reaches of humanity. Preserving our majesty. Aware of our past. Appreciating our past. Keepers of our past. Visited in the present. Understood for the future.

Engage the
Experience

Experience is not
what happens to a
man. It is what a
man does with what
happens to him.
Aldous Huxley

We encounter, confront, touch. We love, be-friend, relate. We laugh, play, enjoy. We lis-ten, communicate, enrich. We endure, persist, continue. Our experience is our joy, our educa-tion, our day. Travel is experience upon experi-ence linked together by the path of our journey. The experience of travel is our cycle. The cycle is our experience.

Experience begets insight. Insight bears wisdom. Insight and wisdom founded in expe-rience, the actual physical, emotional, and sen-sual experience of travel. What do we seek most out of our exceptional experience of travel?

We Find Our Rhythm

We gather momentum as we go. Travel drives us ahead. The more we travel, the greater our vigor. Travel provides the enthusiasm, our vitality, our zest. Travel has its own energy, addictive energy, thrusting us forward. Travel propels us through experience. Travel propels us through the lives of others, through their rhythm. We follow their schedule, their sense of time. Faster. Slower. Their tempo. We follow their rhythm.

We follow the rhythm of the day. We follow the rhythm of the road. We follow the rhythm of the city. We follow the rhythm of nature. We follow the rhythm of ourselves. Our own natural rhythm.

Travel is our catalyst. Travel sets the pace. We embrace the rhythm of travel, its soothing, alluring, organic cadence. We find our rhythm, our own natural, organic flow.

The Fuller Spectrum of Our Daily Choices

Away from our normal lives and routines, we must determine everyday things afresh. We are conscious of the processes of our regular existence. We are cognizant of our daily experiences, acutely aware of what it is that we actually do in our day.

We recognize our habits. How we act, how we sleep, how we eat. How, when, and where. What we do. And what we don't do.

Deprived of the comforts and familiarities of Home, we discover the liberty of choice in our daily life. We discover what we like and what we don't like, what we miss the most. We discover opportunities for change, the potential for change, the potential of change. We discover what we would most like to change. We discover the fuller possibilities of our daily life. We feel splendidly and passionately alive in the fuller spectrum of our daily choices.

We Observe

We are not of the places we visit. We float into the everyday lives of the visited. We observe from a distance, noting that which they may not. We pay attention.

We resort to extraordinary means of understanding. We wonder at how quickly our observational powers sharpen and intensify. We read people quickly, simply, instinctively. We rely on body language, fleeting body signals, an aura around somebody, some place.

We are forced to make instantaneous judgments based on nothing more than a few telling strands of observation. We may be right. We may be dead wrong. But we forgive ourselves. We are forgiven. We are understood. We try to understand.

What is the hardest to convey without words? When did we say the least and understand the most?

We welcome our powers of observation. We celebrate the communication of travel. We master its challenge.

This Versus That

We look for the familiar. We equate. We distinguish. We contrast. Foods, places, people, smells, natural phenomena.

This is better. That was better. This is tastier, stronger, richer, prettier, warmer, colder, friendlier, bigger, grander, more impressive.

"It's just like . . ." "There's no comparison." "Are you kidding?" We agree. We disagree. We assert our likes and dislikes.

We acknowledge our natural human impulse to try to seek some understanding. To impose some order on the massive amounts of information to which we are exposed. To reach out for the guiding light of the known, our known. Simply put, to compare, this versus that.

Behold Our Similarity

Travel trumpets our collective nature. We are astounded by our inherent affinity. Our common needs, desires, pursuits. Our concerns and our joy. Our love and our fears. Our delight and our pain. Our hopes and dreams. Our struggles and celebrations.

Which human qualities are most universal? What aspect of our collective soul gives us the most comfort? And the most concern?

We move beyond our small world into the bigger world, and we know that the bigger world is indeed a "small, small world." Travel offers us the harmony of humanity, the richness of our kind. The vast bond of Us.

Travel Cuts to the Extreme

Travel reveals the best of the best, the worst of the worst. We witness striking splendor and abject poverty in the space of a moment's travel. We witness rawness, searing rawness, captivating our naked eyes. Travel exposes life.

Images of the best of the best come to mind. And then, the worst of the worst. Images and experiences. Experiences and images.

Expecting beauty, we feel pain. Envisioning pain, we encounter beauty. Expecting beauty, we are blessed with indescribable beauty. Envisioning pain, we endure unspeakable pain. We experience travel's extremes. We digest and try to understand its extremes, life's extremes. We welcome the discourse of travel, the discourse of life.

Growth

We Are Fluid

We are prepared for change. We are open to variety, the glorious and fascinating melange that is humanity. Travel keeps us in a rhythm of reevaluation, self-evaluation.

What was once a rule becomes merely a guideline. What was once a guideline becomes one possible approach, of many. Plans change, and so do we.

The adamant yield. The unbending bend. Rigidity releases its hold, its suffocating strangle. Firmness gives way to flexibility, freedom. We invite the open road, the open Us. We surrender. We are open, powerfully open to our travels. Open to others. Open to Us.

Other Ways

<blockquote>
If we are always
arriving and
departing, it is also
true that we are
eternally anchored.
One's destination is
never a place but
rather a new way of
looking at things.
Henry Miller
</blockquote>

Travel changes the way we think, the way we talk, the way we laugh. The way we eat, the way we interact, the way we live.

We learn that there are many different and diverse beliefs, approaches, views. We learn to trust other people and other cultures. We learn that there are alternative approaches to life and that while we may be comfortable with the ways of Home, there is splendor in discovering fresh systems and conventions for living.

What at first seems bizarre and even untenable becomes familiar, acceptable, better than what was. We embrace the peculiar, the unconventional. We celebrate the range of assorted customs, practices, and manners. We laud the diversity of humanity presented by travel's path.

We Reassess

We confront our long-held values and beliefs in the face of a barrage of challenges. We are forced to reexamine our ideas of what's right and what's wrong, what works and what doesn't work, from a clearer, fresher perspective.

We reconcile our opinions. We reconsider our impressions of others. We accommodate our new understanding. We rethink our concepts of life, our philosophies for living. We develop a new creed, based on the fuller, more rounded wisdom of our travels.

Travel Sets Us Free

We are released from the expectations of Home, expectations of who and what we are. From the set of prohibitions and repressions which at first seem to represent what is *normal* but which in fact keep us from a world of untold possibilities—the infinite permutations of Us, who we are, who we can be.

Who is the possible Us? Do we let ourselves meet travel's potential Us?

Travel offers us fresh points of reference, bold possibilities. We are identified with our travel plan, the map of our journey, the course of our wanderings. We are where we are coming from, where we are, and where we are going. We are a new Us. We are free. We embrace the possible Us.

A Clean Slate

Travel allows us to lose ourselves along the way, to know nothing and nobody. Travel lets us lift the burden, our load, our unwanted baggage. We clear our plate. The albatross is removed and thrown away.

Are we comfortable with our open slate? Or does it make us anxious? Are we able to float freely in the weightlessness of travel? What's stopping us? What are we still holding on to?

We start anew. Who are we? Let us find out. Let us discover slowly. We are who we want to be, who we really want to be, who we really are. We float towards Us. Our journey will take us there. We delight in our weightlessness. We are on an open path, a clear, vibrant path.

Our Many Selves

Travel permits us to redefine ourselves in the flux of movement in an effort to understand all that we pass through. We leave behind our Home selves and welcome the momentum of our Moving selves. As we float like a feather from person to person, place to place, through ever-changing environments, we are free to reinvent ourselves, to rediscover ourselves, to explore our many facets.

Travel unveils aspects of our character long hidden. Our courage. Our perseverance. Our humor. Our determination. Our ability to care. Our ability to love.

We think of the best that travel brings out in us. The other sides we still would like to reveal, rediscover.

We peel back layers and explore and discover, inside and out. We experience ourselves, our true selves, perhaps for the first time. We revel in our diverse and powerful Self.

We Trust Our Intuition

We revisit our instinctive Self. We reacquaint ourselves with our *feelings* about people, about places. That little voice inside all of us that tells us what we need to know, what we need to do. That inkling.

We experience life in our gut, at the core. Travel forces us to place trust in our voice, in our sense of things. Whom to trust. Where to go. How to get there.

We learn to trust our intuitive Self, again. We learn to trust our feelings again. We learn to trust our responses, again. As a child who goes forth without knowing, trusting others, and ourselves.

Event. Reflex. Response. Event. Reflex. Response. Event. Reflex. Response. Trust.

We reestablish our connection to the world, to Us. The connection to who we are instinctively. Unconscious, organic. The more we travel, the more we trust. We trust our gift. The gift of our travels. The gift within.

Live Our
Creativity

Our travels are mobile manifestations of our essence. Imaginative, original expressions of our moving being. Evolving displays of our aesthetic, our ambitious, unique vision. Each minute of each hour of each traveling day proclaims our creative, artistic product. The result of our enterprising, inventive, courageous Self.

Empowered by fresh perspectives and a world of possibilities, we expand our creativity, enhance its extent. We see things we never have seen, imagine things we never could have imagined. Sparks, flashes, sudden streaks of profound inspiration. We step beyond, into a broader sense of what can be.

We live the rich colors of our life's creativity, its bold composition, its richly layered texture. A traveling exhibition of our life's pursuits. Travel as art. Our life as art.

Travel Purifies Our Being

What do you suppose will satisfy the Soul, except to walk free...?
Walt Whitman

Like a sculptor, travel removes the surrounding rock to reveal our Essence. With each nick, with each chip that falls away, travel eliminates our debris. Travel carves out our Nature.

We encounter. We make choices. We act and react. We interact. With each mile, with each step, travel exposes us to the light. Travel cleanses our character. Travel etches its reality on our soul. Travel makes us pure. Travel makes us genuine. Travel makes us whole.

We Celebrate Our Core

Travel declares who we are. Relieved of the pressures of our *normal* lives and bombarded by change, we are bared open.

Open to escape. Open to freedom. Open to the world. Open to ourselves. Open to our desires. Open to recognizing and understanding our real needs, our deepest needs. Open to our voice, our core voice, screaming to be heard, screaming to be given a shot at life.

Open to our creativity. Open to our power. Open to rejoicing in the revelations of our travels, in the revelations of our power, travel's power. We applaud Us, our core Us.

What part of Us is calling? We listen carefully, to our Core, our core Us. And celebrate.

The Best Us

Stripped of our unwanted personas, facing our fears and trepidations, embracing our strengths and the abundance around us, our *best* best rises to the top. When has travel shown us our *best* best, the honest essence of who we are and what we seek to be?

We seize glimpses of our true identity. We evolve. We unfold, materialize, take shape. A fuller Us emerges. A buoyant Us. A richer, deeper, rounder image of Us. Lighthearted. Carefree. Truer. Free. We are our purest Self. Our best core Self. Freedom at its finest.

Travel Is Transformative

Whether we travel for a day, a week, or a year, travel presents us with the opportunity to change ourselves in fundamental ways. Travel has the potential to alter us in essential steps, large and small. We are able to look at life from different angles, openly and freely.

We recognize how travel has transformed us. We witness how it has transformed others.

We leave with curiosity, hesitation, and fear. We return with boldness, courage, and wisdom. Travel is affirming, empowering, augmenting. Travel affords us the chance to rejuvenate, to revitalize, to recenter. We return replenished, reinvigorated, restored to our fuller Self.

Healing

We allow the therapy of our ways. We feel motion's therapy. We savor its panacea. We are rescued from stagnancy and boredom. We are free to heal, free to wake up.

Travel is therapy in its purest and most direct form. No substitutions. It's what we want to do, and we do it. It's being where we want to be, in motion. Synthesis.

In motion, we gain perspective, a sense of ourselves, and a sense of our place in the larger world. The journey is engaging and powerful. The journey is our therapy. The journey is healing.

The journey is freedom. The journey is discovery. The journey is encounter. The journey is joy. The journey is challenge. The journey is insight. The journey is growth. The journey is balance. The journey is our road to Us.

Savor the Power

Return

We head Home. We feel the compression of time, the thrust of our journey back to a place that was, from places that are. From places wedged in the forefront of our mind, in the foray of our experiences.

We encounter those who are just going, just heading out. We recount our stories, impart our wisdom. We are the graduating class. Those "in the know." Those who have been.

We quietly think back on our travels, searing each detail into the permanence that is Us. We hold sacred our excursions, our trips, our journeys. We exalt in our sense of accomplishment, strength, fulfillment. We are thankful for our joys, our discoveries, our rediscoveries. We are grateful for our insights, our inspiration, our bliss.

Arrival

The known is calling. Through our window, the familiar appears, beckons, sharpens into focus.

We hesitate. We are wary. And excited. Cautious. And anticipating. The strange mixture of emotions that is Arrival. What goes through our mind in the moments before our arrival? What medley of emotions are we feeling?

And then, we are there. Here. Returned. Home. We welcome our arrival. We approach the familiar. We embrace our family, our friends, our Self. We embrace our journey.

A New Perspective

*We shall not cease
from exploration
And the end of all
our exploring
Will be to arrive
where we started
And know the place
for the first time.*

T. S. Eliot

We're back. Back to reality. A fresh reality. A different reality. Different from the one we left behind.

So much seems to have changed. People, places, the discussion at the table. Not the way we remember it. We see things with different eyes, traveler's eyes. We notice things we once overlooked. We talk with people we once ignored. We visit places we once neglected. We listen to viewpoints we once dismissed.

We're sensitized to our own environment. We are alive, alive at Home. A new place, a new road. We do not drift back to our old ways. We bask in the glorious light of our travels.

We Share Our Travels

We want to share it all, with everybody, with anybody. With those who didn't see what we saw, didn't hear what we heard, didn't smell what we smelled. With those who didn't taste what we tasted, didn't feel what we felt, didn't touch what we touched. With those who didn't understand what we came to understand, didn't meet the people we met, didn't share our dreams. Our actualized dreams, our new reality, our unique journey.

We regale them with stories of serendipity. We recount our tales of adventure. We show our slides, photographs, and videos to others. To ourselves. Again and again. To recapture, to revisit, to relive our experiences.

Who will best understand what we have experienced? Out of all our many adventures, tales, and insights, what will they connect with most?

We want to share it out loud, for all our friends, colleagues, and relatives to hear: "Travel, travel, travel!"

We Stand Apart

We experience a parting of experience, a duality of paths, a divergence of sensitivities. We hold on to exotic notions. We prefer romantic concepts of life. We seem odd, unconventional, bizarre. Our reality appears peculiar, curious, absurd.

And yet our new reality is understood and accepted as an essential part of Us, as a critical part of our journey, our imagination, our dreams. In deference to where we've been, whom we've met. Reverence for what we've experienced. For now.

The Wonders of Home

We incorporate the spirit of our travels into our everyday life. We integrate travel into our experiences, our attitudes.

We explore Home. We discover the greatness of the everyday, the grandeur of the simple things. A walk, a conversation, a bus ride into town. We sign up for a class at a local college. We learn a new language, a new recipe. We take in a play, read a new book. We chat with our neighbors, with our grocer. We enjoy a lunch-hour concert in the park.

We appreciate Home. A comfy couch in which to fall asleep. A kitchen in which to conjure up a glorious meal for friends and family, some local delicacy we picked up along the way. A garden in which to tend our perennials. A local pub "where everybody knows our name."

We venture out, into the world that surrounds us every day, filled with a new sense of marvel. We compare. We distinguish. A quarry to be mined, to be prospected, to be revealed.

Cherish Our Travels

We hold our journey holy. We replay it in our mind over and over, lest one second, one moment, trickle out. We read and reread our diaries, our journals. We daydream of what was. And what will be again.

We feel ourselves on that bus, on that plane, in that dugout canoe. We envision ourselves There. Back There. On that windswept coast in Oregon. At that gelateria in Rome. On that camel's back in Jaiselmer.

We hold on to the uniqueness of our journey. We revere the rapture of our motion, the excitement and adventure of our movement. Travel resonates in our soul. We are thankful for its course.

We Own Our Experiences for Eternity

Travel preserves our desires, our longings, our ventures. Travel allows us to possess the world. We own our steps, our path, our direction. We own our passion. We seize our dreams and capture time in our heart.

Held up to the litmus test of life, each travel moment is sacred, eternal. Good or bad, each day is treasured, remembered, embraced. We take with us the places we've been and the people we've met as essential parts of our soul, permanent threads in our fabric. The lessons of travel guide us through life, enduring, timeless. We laud our boldness, our courage, our journey.

Enlightenment Is Within

The events in our lives happen in a sequence in time, but in their significance to ourselves, they find their own order . . . the continuous thread of revelation.

Eudora Welty

We have seen so much. We have done so much. We have experienced so much. We have felt things most others haven't. Most others don't. Most others won't. We have explored and discovered, ventured and loved. We have enriched and enjoyed, given and received. We have informed our mind and illuminated our heart.

But the truths of our experiences are buried richly in our being, surfacing in choice, fleeting moments of understanding and clarity. Precious seconds shedding light on the scope of our travel's path. Shining, dazzling comets of glowing, penetrating insight. From lands afar and deep within.

More Power

We Fuel Our
Passion

We feed our travel fire. We read about places we've visited and places still to go. We check out the travel section of our newspaper and surf travel sites on the Internet. We grab coffee with friends, and chat and reminisce.

We spend a moment at a train station, a bus terminal, or an airport and long for what lies at the other end.

We pass a traveler and offer some assistance. Are you lost? Where are you heading? Can we take you there? We understand. We've been there.

We walk by a travel agency. And stop. And look in, through the window. And through the door.

We take little trips. We plan our next big trip. We sustain our desire. We nourish and support our travel dreams.

Leave Again.
And Again

Travel is addictive. Wonderfully, magically habit forming. Being in one place without going anywhere, without traveling, scares us, suffocates us. We feel claustrophobic, imprisoned. We need to go. We go. Again. Travel calls.

It's been too long since our last break. A little voice says we need to go. We go. Again. Travel calls.

We are invested with movement. We make lists of new places to go. To where? We don't know. Everywhere. Anywhere.

We go. We return. Go and return. A cycle, a cycle that takes us from Home to travel and back again. And again.

We learn to recognize our rooted side, our motion side, our wandering side. We learn to nurture and care for our rooted side, our motion side, our wandering side. We pay attention to both Home and Away. We are committed to balancing life's journey. We are permitted to leave again. And again.

Each Journey Anew

Every trip offers another perspective. Places change. People change. We change. Different places at different times in our life. Different circumstances. Different situations. Different emotions. We grow with each voyage, each excursion, each new venture. Each new chapter in our travels.

What we once dismissed, now takes on interest, fascination. What was once of interest, we now dismiss. Travel illustrates our evolving appreciation of others and ourselves. Our evolving likes and dislikes. Our evolving tolerance and intolerance. Our evolving sense of joy and intrigue, wonder and splendor. Our ever-changing passions. Travel embodies our transformation over days, weeks, years. Over our lifetime.

No Endings, Only Beginnings

Our travels continue. In our mind, in our soul. In our humanity.

Vacations and voyages. Jaunts and journeys. Remarkable, never-ending episodes in our life. Vibrant and captivating. Motivating and encouraging. Healing and teaching. Driving and resting our spirits. Centering. Sources of inspiration in the pursuit of being the best we can be. We extol travel's perpetual seam, its endless genesis.

Go!

Go and see. Go and look. Go and observe. Go and witness. Go and search. Go and explore. Go and listen. Go and discover. Go and rediscover. Go and Answer. Go and compare. Go and learn. Go and reassess. Go and understand. Go and expand. Go and express. Go and create. Go and be open. Go and cherish.

Go and have fun. Go and encounter. Go and eat. Go and converse. Go and share. Go and sing. Go and deserve. Go and delight. Go and nurture. Go and enrich. Go and give. Go and reveal. Go and behold. Go and befriend. Go and love. Go and welcome. Go and respect. Go and embrace. Go and treasure. Go and be joyous. Go and live the adventure.

Go and release. Go and receive. Go and challenge. Go and take risks. Go and move through. Go and experience. Go and absorb. Go and capture. Go and choose. Go and do. Go and grow. Go and heal. Go and be free. Go and own. Go and live. Go and transform. Go and purify. Go and return. Go and stand apart. Go and savor. Go and be the best. Go and be. Go and soar.

Go. Go now. Go and go again. Go and travel. Travel and celebrate life.

A Prayer for
the Traveler

Let the road resonate.
Let the mysterious captivate.
Let acceptance abound.

Let imagination seduce.
Let patience teem.
Let joy reign.

Let surrender capture.
Let trust preside.
Let abundance provide.

Let curiosity consume.
Let wonder mesmerize.
Let life surprise.

Let dreams sail
Let passion prevail.
Let travel triumph!

Gratitude

The power of travel is a tapestry woven with the energy of many magical souls illuminating the path. I honor the radiance of these resplendent beacons:

Thelma and Joel Zikman, for engendering the journey and for being there at all the crossroads;

Lisa Carnio, Annette Du Toit, Mark Haslam, Laurie Kinerk, Jeremy and Gayle Pope, Ward Prystay, and Linda Weech, for sharing the journey;

Susan Zikman and Janice Gritti, for their endless laughter and love on the circuit of life;

Barbara Freeman, for her ever-present enthusiasm to explore the exotic frontier between family and friendship;

Marcus Brewster, Leigh Flayton, Andrew London, Nancy Mills, Pattie O'Leary, and Susan Rogers, for their gracious tips and spacious suggestions;

Rob Fung, for the depth and breadth of his faith, encouragement, and caring heart;

Lea Freeman, for answering the call of my earliest wanderlust and sharing a lifetime of wisdom;

Shirlee and Hymie Fleischer, Patricia Hands, Theresa Lewis, and Nomi Morris, for providing a home away from home;

My colleagues at Goodman and Carr, for entrusting their travel dreams;

Jack Canfield and Kim Kirberger, for their panoramic plains and generosity of vision;

Karen Bouris and Marc Labinger, for pointing me towards the horizon;

Susan Schulman, for being a warm and nurturing compass in the vastness of new lands;

David Groff, for his receptivity and intuitive sense of direction;

Joel Fotinos, for his clarity in embracing the open sky.

And a special postcard of appreciation to Cape Town, for embodying the brilliance of place and for centering me when I needed it most.

Send Us Your Powerful Stories

D o you wish to share a story or anecdote illustrating how the power of travel has enhanced, enriched, or expanded your life, for potential inclusion in an upcoming book? If so, please send your submissions by e-mail to: **stories@poweroftravel.com**, or by regular mail to:

The Power of Travel
P.O. Box 69774
Los Angeles, California
U.S.A. 90069

If you are using e-mail, we prefer that each submission be sent in the body of the e-mail (not as an attachment) and that you send a separate e-mail message for each submission.

Stories should be less than 1,000 words.

You may submit original unpublished stories or previously published material.

Ensure that you include your name, address, and telephone number on all correspondence. At the top of your submission, please indicate a heading from the book's table of contents (for example, "The Magic of Motion," "Summoning Our Senses," etc.) which best describes your piece. Please keep a copy of your submission, as we are unable to return material.

About the Author

Steve Zikman is a popular keynote speaker, in-house seminar leader, and spokesperson for companies, organizations, professional associations, retreat centers, and educational institutions.

For further information on Steve Zikman's speaking programs and consulting work, or to book Steve for your next conference or in-house event, please e-mail us at **info@ poweroftravel.com** or visit our Web site at **www.poweroftravel.com**.

175